Queen Mary's Dolls' House

OFFICIAL SOUVENIR GUIDE

CW00801726

Contents

Introduction

RIGHT
Miniature state portrait
of Queen Mary by
Sir William Orpen in
the Saloon.

BELOW
The Wisden cricket bat,
from the games cupboard
off the Entrance Hall, set
against a full-size cricket
ball. The house has a full
set of classic English
games equipment.

Queen Mary's Dolls' House is not a dolls' house in the usual sense – that is, it is not a children's toy. Instead, it is a glorified and fully furnished architectural model, created by the great British architect Sir Edwin Lutyens (1869–1944), and is intended to be a historical record of the ideal early twentieth-century English house. It is also meant to be a source of fun. Conceived in 1921, it was a product of the period just after the First World War, when, in reaction to the horrors of the recent past, people wished to escape into a brighter, more frivolous world. The 1920s was the decade of the 'bright young things', and the Dolls' House reflects some of that lightness of spirit.

It is a peculiarly English conceit, being a national monument in the form of a miniature building. It had a serious purpose, as a demonstration of the best of English arts, crafts and manufacturing, as they affected contemporary domestic life. The house was originally a star exhibit at the British Empire Exhibition at Wembley in 1924. This was the first great post-war international

trading exhibition, planned as an advertisement and celebration of the economic products of Britain and her colonies, and intended to promote international trade after the disruption of the war. Many of the components of the Dolls' House are miniature versions of goods from classic British manufacturers of the day, from Wisden cricket bats and Waring & Gillow furniture, to Purdey guns, Rolls-Royce motor cars and even Cooper's Oxford marmalade and Rowntree's sweets. A surprising number of these famous names are still in business today, almost 90 years later, though others have already passed into history.

The house had another long-term purpose. As Lutyens described it:

Let us devise and design for all time something which will enable future generations to see how a king and queen of England lived in the twentieth century, and what authors, artists and craftsmen of note there were during their reign.

The aim was to present a little model house of the early twentieth century, fitted out with perfect fidelity down to the smallest details, such as kitchen provisions and even lavatory paper in the bathrooms. It was

OPPOSITE
The top of one of the folio
cabinets in the Library,
with an array of miniature
objects, including cigars,
matches and a pipe for
the smoker, a statue of
Napoleon in characteristic
pose, and the two
Purdey guns.

intended to represent a genuine and complete example of a domestic interior, with household arrangements characteristic of contemporary life, to provide an interesting record for the future. In the words of the writer A.C. Benson (1862–1925), who edited the official two-volume history of the house published in 1924:

if we suppose that the present Queen's House lasts on for, say, two hundred years, the little mansion which seems positively the last word in convenience and beauty … our successors will look at [it] in astonishment, and wonder that men could ever have deigned to live in so laborious and cumbrous a way … But at the same time, how they will value the House as an historical document.

LEFT
The passenger lift, with mahogany and mirror interior. The house contains two electric lifts (the other is for luggage), both made by Otis and capable of working. The lift cables are made of fine fishing line.

BELOW
A pair of Purdey shotguns and their miniature cartridges against a real cartridge. King George V was so pleased with these guns that he asked for them to be displayed on top of one of the folio cabinets in the Library, rather than placed out of sight in the gun cupboard.

BELOW
King George V and Queen Mary in Coronation Robes, 22 June 1911.

Now that it is well on the way to becoming a hundred years old, this is perhaps the principal interest of the house – as an untouched example of the taste in interior decoration and the contents of a rich house of that period. However, it was already something of an anachronism when it was built. Although its promoters in 1921–4 spoke of it as a model and record of a contemporary house, it is really an Edwardian or pre-war house. Lutyens and his architectural contemporaries would have had few chances to build a real house like this in the changed economic circumstances after the First World War. This gives Queen Mary's Dolls' House a particular poignancy as an architectural record.

Primarily, however, the Dolls' House was conceived as a national tribute to the royal family, in the form of a gift to Queen Mary (1867–1953), as a sign of the affection in which she and her husband King George V (r.1910–36) were held, and in acknowledgement of their steadfast leadership during the war. Everything in the house was a present, whether from the artists, craftsmen and manufacturers who made its contents, or from individuals who made small donations to pay for particular aspects of the work. Queen Mary herself, when she wrote in 1924 to thank all those who had been involved, described it as 'the most perfect present that anyone could receive'.

PRINCESS MARIE LOUISE

The house was the brainchild of Princess Marie Louise (1872–1956), a first cousin of King George V and the youngest daughter of Queen Victoria's (r.1837–1901) fifth child, Princess Helena (1846–1923), and Prince Christian of Schleswig-Holstein (1831–1917). Princess Marie Louise had been a childhood friend of Queen Mary and was a great favourite of King George V. Her marriage to a prince of Anhalt had ended in annulment, and by the 1920s she was living with her family at Cumberland Lodge in Windsor Great Park, a grace-and-favour residence. The Princess was interested in books, music and the arts, and her personal circle of friends was drawn from that milieu.

At Easter in 1921, when the Court was at

ABOVE

Josefine Swoboda (1861–1924), *Princess Marie Louise of Schleswig-Holstein*, 1891. Princess Marie Louise was a granddaughter of Queen Victoria and first cousin of King George V.

ABOVE
Lutyens was fond of
illustrating his letters
to the Princess, as this
doodle from a letter of
1921 shows. He wrote:
'O! I saw one of your
gentlemen footmen
today outside your
Highness's Palace!'

Windsor, Princess Marie Louise had spent the day with the King and Queen at the Castle, where they had shown her much kindness. When she returned home to Cumberland Lodge, she found her mother and sister assembling a collection of miniature furniture for Queen Mary. The Queen's greatest enthusiasm was for old furniture and interior decoration, and she was an avid collector of 'antiques'. She also had a particular passion for miniature objects: Fabergé animals, oriental hardstone carvings, children's silver furniture, eighteenth-century cabinet-makers' apprenticeship models and similar examples of 'tiny craft', which she displayed in specially made glass cabinets in the private rooms of the royal palaces. This gave Princess Marie Louise an idea. She announced to her family that she would commission a dolls' house as a present for the Queen.

The idea might have been no more than an eccentric whimsy, but because of Princess Marie Louise's friendships in literary and artistic circles, she was able to involve a number of eminent figures in the project, in particular the greatest architect of the age, Sir Edwin Lutyens. It was Lutyens's genius that transformed the project and made it into the extraordinary work of art that was eventually achieved. At the Royal Academy Summer Exhibition that year, Princess Marie Louise approached Lutyens and asked him if he would do her a favour. Intrigued, Lutyens asked what it was. To design a dolls' house for Queen Mary, she replied. Other architects of his stature, or indeed those of lesser ability but with

more pompous self-regard, might have reacted differently. Lutyens, however, agreed immediately and enthusiastically.

Lutyens himself had an element of the child about him, and a particular streak of playfulness in his artistic make-up. His own engagement present to his future wife, Lady Emily Bulwer-Lytton (1874–1964), in 1896, had been an elaborate casket, containing, among other things, the miniature plans for their ideal home. At the Liverpool Catholic Cathedral (his never-completed final masterpiece), he designed the banisters of the stairs down to the crypt to make it easy for choir boys to slide down them. The idea of designing a dolls' house would have appealed to his playful, childlike streak.

It would also have tickled his sense of humour. As part of his greatest scheme, the capital of India at New Delhi, begun in 1912, Lutyens was working contemporaneously on the palatial Viceroy's House. This was the largest house of the time. It would have amused Lutyens to have received a commission for the smallest, too. He had a very pronounced, if sometimes startling, sense of humour: genial, whimsical, disconcerting, irreverent and facetious. When Montagu Norman, the governor of the Bank of England, showed Lutyens into the hallowed Court Room (where the financial destiny of the world had been controlled for two centuries), he broke into a two-step and exclaimed, 'Just the place for a *thé dansant*.' (He did not subsequently receive the commission to reconstruct the Bank of England.)

BELOW
In a letter of 1921 to
Princess Marie Louise,
Sir Arthur Cope outlines
his plans for a portrait of
Queen Mary, including
this rough sketch.

SIR EDWIN LUTYENS

Sir Edwin Lutyens (knighted in 1918) was the architect *par excellence* of the era of King George V, responsible for public memorials to the First World War (notably the Cenotaph in Whitehall and the great Arch at Thiepval on the Somme), prestigious buildings in the City of London and the British Embassy in Washington, as well as New Delhi. He had originally established his name as a designer of houses in Surrey in the 1890s and early 1900s, following in the steps of Philip Webb (1831–1915), Norman Shaw (1831–1912) and his old master (in whose office he had trained), Sir Ernest George (1839–1922). His work went through a number of phases; during the Edwardian period it developed from his earlier Surrey Arts and Crafts manner to a refined and original classicism, inspired by the English seventeenth century and the work of Inigo Jones (1573–1652) and Sir Christopher Wren (1632–1723), and the masters of the High Renaissance in Rome – Bramante, Sangallo, Peruzzi and Michelangelo. The Dolls' House is a product of this later mood, with many resonances from the work of Lutyens's architectural heroes.

Lutyens, born in 1869, was the eleventh of 14 children of Captain Charles Henry Augustus Lutyens, an officer in the Lancashire Fusiliers. Originally merchants from the Baltic, who had settled in England in the early eighteenth century, the Lutyenses also had an artistic streak. Lutyens's father had made a reputation for himself as a painter of fox-hunting subjects and landscapes, and divided his time between London and Surrey. Family friends

included well-known artists, such as the children's illustrator Randolph Caldecott (1846–86), who taught Lutyens to sketch old vernacular buildings, and Sir Edwin Landseer (1802–73), one of Queen Victoria's favourite artists, after whom Lutyens was named. A delicate child, he was educated mainly at home and in London day schools. It was not surprising, therefore, that Lutyens followed his artistic bent. He later told the writer Sir Osbert Sitwell (1892–1959):

Any talent I may have had was due to long illness as a boy, which afforded me time to think, and to subsequent ill-health, because I was not allowed to play games, and so had to teach myself, for my enjoyment, to use my eyes instead of my feet.

LEFT
Sir William Rothenstein (1872–1945), *Sir Edwin Lutyens*, 1922. This portrait of the architect is one of several hundred miniature works of art commissioned for the house. Frank Lloyd Wright (1857–1969), one of America's most important twentieth-century architects and a contemporary of Lutyens, paid a notable tribute to the designer of the Dolls' House, voicing 'admiration for the love, loyalty and art with which this cultured architect, in love with Architecture, shaped his buildings ... Nor can I think of anyone able to so characteristically and quietly dramatise the old English feeling for dignity and comfort in an interior, however or wherever that interior might be in England.'

BELOW
Sir William Nicholson,
Gertrude Jekyll, 1920.
Lutyens benefited from
the encouragement of
his Surrey neighbours,
especially the famous
gardener Miss Gertrude
Jekyll (1843–1932), for
whom he designed
Munstead Wood, her
house near Godalming.
Jekyll's horticultural
innovations revolutionised
the English approach to
gardening. Miss Jekyll,
who was memorably
described by the writer
Logan Pearsall Smith as
looking like 'some ancient
incredibly aristocratic
denizen of a river jungle,
gazing gravely out from
the tangled reeds', was a
great influence on the
young Lutyens, and
worked frequently with
him on the design of the
gardens that formed an
integral aspect of his
new houses.

LEFT
The Garden by Gertrude
Jekyll, one of the
miniature volumes from
the Dolls' House Library,
photographed on a classic
Lutyens bench in the
Garden. As well as
designing the Garden
itself, Miss Jekyll also
contributed a copy of her
great work on garden
design to the leather-
bound miniature volumes
in the Library.

Architecture was the perfect field for Lutyens's particular talents for mathematics, drawing and observation, combined with an extraordinary visual memory, inherited traits that, in his case, were said to be combined with a creative imagination of genius.

After studying architecture for two years at the South Kensington Schools (later the Royal College of Art), where the fashionable Arts and Crafts architect and protégé of Ruskin's, Detmar Blow (1867–1939), was a contemporary, Lutyens obtained a place in the 'Eton of Offices', that of the architects George and Peto. However, he stayed there for only a year before precociously setting up in independent practice in 1889, aged 20.

Lutyens became widely accepted in his own lifetime as one of the greatest, if not the greatest English architect. Christopher Hussey (1899–1970), in his biography of the architect, wrote:

The genius of Lutyens was a legend that dawned on the early Edwardians, had become a portent before the First World War, and remained a fixed star in the architectural firmament, despite the rising of the constellation of Le Corbusier, until his death on New Year's Day 1944 … In his lifetime he was widely held to be our greatest architect since Wren, if not, as many maintained, his superior … [Lutyens's buildings] exceeded in quantity any noted designer in these or other days and by their variety and distinction almost defy classification … He had his amazing capacity to project his imagination into every space of whatever he was building, so that he lived the life of the people who would ultimately inhabit it, more vividly perhaps than they ever would themselves, and in a sense became the building.

This ability to project himself into his designs stood Lutyens in good stead when presented with a miniature but perfect architectural exercise such as the Dolls' House. Lutyens transformed a miniature curiosity into a serious, albeit irreverent, architectural venture.

THE DOLLS' HOUSE COMMITTEE

The project was blessed with other good luck during its incubation, notably its incorporation into the programme for an Empire trade exhibition of arts and manufacturing in the nineteenth-century tradition – a tradition initiated by the Great Exhibition of 1851. At his first meeting with Princess Marie Louise after the Royal Academy Summer Exhibition, Lutyens brought with him Sir Herbert Morgan, who was President of the Society of Industrial Artists, one of the bodies involved in the government's project for the British Empire Exhibition at Wembley Park, Middlesex, planned for 1924.

Morgan immediately saw the value of the Dolls' House as a miniature display of British craftsmanship and a potentially popular public exhibit in an intended 'Palace of Arts' gallery. The creation of the proposed Dolls' House fitted perfectly into the timetable for the exhibition and gave a deadline and purpose to work towards. The first stage was to establish a wider committee to mastermind the project. Sir Herbert Morgan agreed to host a dinner party at the Savoy Hotel, to which he, Princess Marie Louise and Lutyens invited friends, artists and others whom they thought could be involved.

In the meantime, Princess Marie Louise had broached the subject with Queen Mary, the intended recipient. At first, the Queen was very surprised, but once her artistic and historical sense was fired, she agreed. Queen Mary also gave her permission for

BELOW
Detail of the Corinthian order on the north front of the Dolls' House.

ABOVE
The grand piano
in the Saloon.

the Dolls' House to be displayed in a special gallery at Wembley. A small fee would be charged for admission, the proceeds from which would go towards the fund set up by Queen Mary for her myriad charitable activities, including hospitals, schools, orphanages and the Royal School of Needlework. This added another strand to the project and gave the idea for the eventual permanent display of the Dolls' House at Windsor Castle, where the admission charge (originally 6d, or 2½ pence) would also augment the Queen's Fund. Queen Mary asked Princess Marie Louise to act as her personal intermediary between Lutyens and the others involved, so that she could be kept informed of progress. In the event, she took the keenest direct interest in the scheme, often visiting the Dolls' House while it was being constructed and fitted out.

At the Savoy dinner, where Sir Herbert Morgan was confirmed as chairman of the committee, the promoters received an enthusiastic response, and the idea crystallised of the house being a permanent record of contemporary domestic design. In her memoirs, Princess Marie Louise recorded how Lutyens started to produce plans and designs for the house, drawing on the menus, napkins and tablecloth. That initial sketched-out scheme was, with few modifications, to become the design of the house as built. The principal change was to be the replacement of the Ionic order of architecture for the house by the richer and more decorative Corinthian. It was not to be a palace, with public rooms for ceremonial, or offices for the departments of the household, but a 'gentleman's house', with royal touches and allusions, such as the royal family might have used as their private home. It was also agreed that the work would be paid for by lots of small 'gifts and private donations', and not by large-scale fund-raising. A three-year timetable was fixed for the project.

Another key figure enlisted at the Savoy dinner was Sir Lawrence Weaver, architectural editor of *Country Life*, who was also the Director Designate of the United Kingdom exhibits at the Wembley Exhibition, and responsible for integrating the Dolls' House into the display scheme there. He was also to play a large role in the interior fitting of the house, masterminding the furnishings. It is largely due to Weaver, together with the furniture historian and writer Percy Macquoid (1852–1925), who also gave advice, that the interior of the house is such a faithful representation of the cultivated taste of the time, and of the early twentieth-century approach to antique furniture and the arrangement of rooms

ABOVE
Sir Lawrence Weaver (1876–1930), Director Designate of the United Kingdom exhibits at the Wembley Exhibition, was responsible for incorporating the Dolls' House into the Palace of Arts there, where it was visited by well over 1.5 million people in seven months.

ABOVE
Wooden model of Lutyens's unexecuted design for the Metropolitan Cathedral of Christ the King in Liverpool. The model is now displayed at the Museum of Liverpool.

RIGHT
The dolls' house from
Uppark, created *c.*1735.
Elaborately furnished
dolls' houses like this one
were an inspiration for
Queen Mary's Dolls'
House.

– what might almost be called, in retrospect, 'Queen Mary taste'. The Dolls' House is already a record of this vanishing style, which, until recently, could still be widely savoured in National Trust properties and other houses open to the public, but which has now generally given way to a more 'historically authentic' approach to old furniture and decoration.

It was Weaver's and Lutyens's decision that everything in the house should be specifically commissioned to a uniform scale of one inch to a foot (that is, 2.5 centimetres to 30.5 centimetres, or a scale of 1:12). Some older objects were integrated into its furnishings, but, on the whole, the donation of any old miniature pieces was discouraged. Much of the furniture was to be copied from famous examples in English private collections – a chandelier from Knole, beds and clocks at Hampton Court Palace, chairs at Harewood House, a lacquer cabinet from Londonderry House. Scaled-down models of Lutyens's own designs for furniture were also used, as in the Kitchen of the Dolls' House, or the Broadwood grand piano in the Saloon, which was based on one designed by Lutyens for the British Pavilion at the Paris Exhibition in 1900.

Just a few weeks after the Savoy dinner, Lutyens had worked up his initial sketch into a complete set of scaled plans and elevations, just like those for a proper building. He also coordinated the team of 1,500 craftsmen, artists and tradesmen responsible for executing the work, and took responsibility for much of the financing – guaranteeing up to £11,000 of his own money – until the individual donations came in. After the repayment in 1924 of the £6,300 that he had spent, he confessed to his wife that he had been 'rather fearful of death before repayment as it would have hit me badly'.

The structure of the house was made by Parnell & Son of Rugby, using Lutyens's plans, just as they would have done if erecting a real building or an architect's model. In this way, the house forms a domestic pendant to the spectacular wooden model of Lutyens's design for the Roman Catholic Cathedral of Liverpool, which is one of the most important architectural models ever created. The tradition of architectural models to scale in wood goes back to the early Renaissance, and many important architectural designs, which were never completed or were superseded, survive now only in this form. Queen Mary's Dolls' House combines this serious design tradition with that of English dolls' houses as fully furnished playthings – the latter reaching its peak in the eighteenth-century examples at Nostell Priory in Yorkshire or Uppark in Sussex. There was a revival of interest in these artefacts in the early twentieth century, as part of the general upsurge of enthusiasm for Georgian art and design.

Once the timber shell of Queen Mary's Dolls' House was completed, it was set up in Lutyens's Delhi office in Apple Tree Yard, Westminster, where artists painted the ceilings, while craftsmen and decorators started work on embellishing and fitting the interior. Clare Nauheim and Beatrice Webb, administrative assistants in Lutyens's office, coordinated the furnishings and liaised with the Master of the Household, Sir Derek Keppel (1863–1944), at Buckingham Palace, over borrowing items such as table linen or royal china for copying to a miniature scale, or arranging access for artists to paint views of the interior of Windsor Castle to hang in

the house. Others were enlisted to help at this stage, such as Lady Jekyll (1861–1937), Gertrude Jekyll's sister-in-law, who was asked to advise on filling the store rooms, and on stocking the Kitchen. She was obviously regarded within the Lutyens circle as an expert on 'domestic science', and even wrote a miniature recipe book, of dishes suitable for dolls, to go in the house.

Reading some of the correspondence, it is possible to deduce an almost pained patience on the part of the military Sir Derek, who, one feels, may have considered that some of the more fanatical concern for accuracy was getting out of hand. Princess Marie Louise herself assumed responsibility for one of the more daring bits of extraction for copying – that of the King's dispatch boxes, used for his official documents. Miniatures of them were to be provided for the desk in the Dolls' House Library (see page 35). On seeing the finished miniatures, King George V asked who had given her permission to copy them. Marie Louise replied that nobody had; she had simply asked for them. The King was surprised, but amused.

ABOVE
Sir Derek Keppel, Master of the Household, 1913–36. Keppel's patient assistance enabled many domestic items at Buckingham Palace to be copied in miniature for the Dolls' House.

BELOW
Miniature copy of one of the King's dispatch boxes.

BELOW
Edward Verrall Lucas
(1868–1938), essayist and
editor, was an old friend
of Princess Marie Louise
and assisted her in the
creation of the Library.

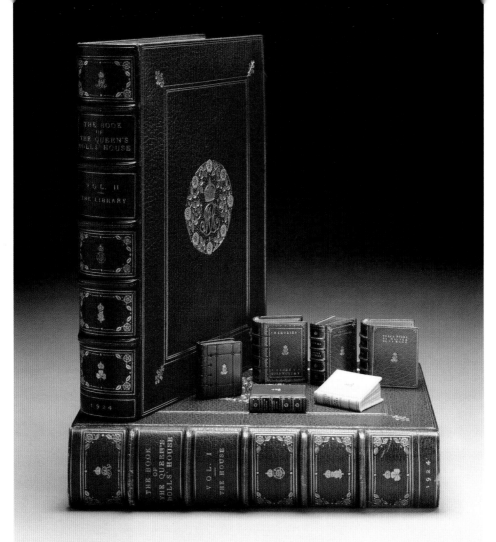

LEFT
*The Book of the Queen's
Dolls' House* and *The
Book of the Queen's Dolls'
House Library*, both
published by Methuen
and Co. Ltd in 1924, with
a selection of minature
volumes from the Library.

THE CREATION OF THE LIBRARY

Princess Marie Louise was also personally responsible for one of the most interesting and important aspects of the whole project, the commissioning of a representative range of works by contemporary authors and artists for the Library – the former in the form of autograph works in tiny bound volumes, and the latter in the form of miniature drawings, watercolours and etchings for two folio cabinets. Lutyens himself presented a tiny set of his plans for the house. In this task, the Princess, as honorary librarian of the house, was assisted by an old friend, the essayist and editor Edward Verrall Lucas, who was a well-known figure in literary circles in the 1920s. Princess Marie Louise wrote letters in her own hand (2,000 in all) to a selection of contemporary talent and had a good response. Even today, with the

ABOVE
Verses written
and illustrated by
Rudyard Kipling
(1865–1936), his
contribution to
the Library.

benefit of hindsight, the miniature Library of the Dolls' House presents a remarkably balanced cross-section of the literary life of the period. It contains works by 171 authors, including such well-known figures as Thomas Hardy, Rudyard Kipling (an unpublished set of verses in his own hand), Arnold Bennett, Hilaire Belloc, G.K. Chesterton, Laurence Binyon, A.E. Housman, Siegfried Sassoon, W.S. Maugham, Sir Arthur Conan Doyle, Edmund Gosse, the Bensons, John Buchan, Aldous Huxley, Ronald Knox, Walter de la Mare, Edmund Blunden, Sir James Barrie and Robert Bridges (then Poet Laureate), as

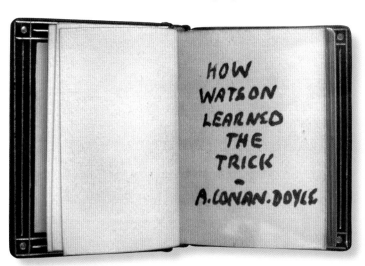

well as lesser, but still remembered names, such as Oscar Browning, H. Rider Haggard, Maurice Baring, Anthony Hope, M.R. James and Mrs Belloc Lowndes. Many of them contributed works specially written for the Dolls' House Library, and all were printed in full in the *Book of the Queen's Dolls' House Library*, compiled by Lucas in 1924 (one of two volumes that formed the official record and history of the house when it was completed).

The authors entered into the spirit of the occasion. Thomas Hardy wrote to Princess

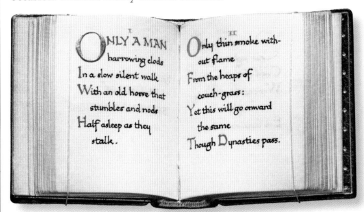

Marie Louise: 'I am much pleased with the look of the miniature book, in which I have put my name. It makes one wish to have a whole library of such books.' Only one author refused to contribute, and 'in a very rude manner' – cranky old George Bernard Shaw. A.E. Housman perhaps summed up the general feeling behind the response in 1923: 'My old, dear and intimate friend Princess Marie Louise, who is furnishing the Queen's Dolls' House, asked me some months ago to let twelve poems of mine be copied small to form one volume in the library; and I selected the twelve shortest and simplest and least likely to fatigue the attention of the dolls or the illustrious

ABOVE
Thomas Hardy
(1840–1928),
'Only a Man', one of nine
poems sent by Hardy.

LEFT
Sir Arthur Conan Doyle
(1859–1930), *How Watson
Learned the Trick*, a
Sherlock Holmes story.

House of Hanover.' G.K. Chesterton referred to the project as a 'national and historic object … I have been only too much honoured to help.' The Library also contained music, including scores by contemporary English composers such as Sir Arthur Bliss, Gustav Holst, Sir Arnold Bax, Hubert Parry and even the noted eccentric Lord Berners. Again there was one notable exception, and, rather surprisingly, that was Sir Edward Elgar. The writer and war poet, Siegfried Sassoon (who did not care for Elgar, having been verbally attacked by him at a party), reported that in a 'crescendo climax of rudeness', Elgar said,

LEFT
Sir William Nicholson (1872–1949), the most distinguished of the artists who contributed to the Dolls' House. As well as miniature paintings, Nicholson was responsible for the murals of the Garden of Eden in the Upper Hall.

BELOW
Miniature music scores by Adela Maddison (c.1862–1929), who organised the Dolls' House music library, and Gustav Holst (1874–1934).

we all know that the King and Queen are incapable of appreciating anything artistic; they have never asked for the full score of my Second Symphony to be added to the library at Windsor. But as the crown of my career I'm asked to contribute to – a Dolls' House for the Queen! … I consider it an insult for an artist to be asked to mix himself up in such nonsense.

Seven hundred artists did get 'mixed up', however, and provided little pictures for the house. They have not all stood the test of time as well as the authors, and many of their names are now almost forgotten. This may be

because the intention was to commission works from across the British Isles, including provincial art centres such as the West of England Academy at Bristol, the Shrewsbury School of Art and Newcastle College of Art, and from the colonies, as well as from established artists in London. There was also a substantial representation of humorous work, which, by its nature, tends to be more

Mark Gertler.

Sigismund Goetze.

FAR LEFT
Mark Gertler (1891–1939),
Head of a woman.

LEFT
Sigismund Goetze
(1866–1939),
My Dear Lady Betty.

BELOW
Sir William Russell Flint
(1880–1969),
A Summer Beach.

ephemeral. In the case of some of the older artists approached, including John Singer Sargent, Charles Ricketts and Charles Haslewood Shannon, their eyesight did not allow them to work on a miniature scale. For whatever reason, some of the most notable early twentieth-century artists are absent from the Dolls' House, though possibly the greatest – Sir William Nicholson – is prominently represented.

The best art in the collection is the mural decoration by Glyn Philpot, Professor R. Anning Bell and Nicholson, or the oil paintings hanging on the walls by Royal Academicians such as Sir Alfred Munnings, Sir John Lavery, Sir William Orpen and Ambrose McEvoy. Etchings and engravings for the folio cabinets were provided by the likes of Burleigh Bruhl,

Talbot Kelly, G.S. Lumsdun, Frank Short and Sidney Tushingham, and Scottish and Irish watercolours by Percy Lancaster, Graham Petrie and Murray Urquhart (whose names are now known mainly to specialists), as well as works by better-known artists, such as Sir William Russell Flint, Mark Gertler, Dame Laura Knight, Paul Nash and Sir William Rothenstein.

W. Russell Flint, R.S.W., R.W.S.

PREPARING THE DOLLS' HOUSE FOR DISPLAY

RIGHT
Sir John Lavery,
*Edward Knoblock, c.*1930.
An American-born
connoisseur, Knoblock
was a leader of the revival
of interest in English
Regency taste and gave
a number of small items
to the Dolls' House,
acquired on his travels
and forays into antique
shops.

As the work progressed, it gathered a momentum of its own and attracted supporters and donors. One such was the connoisseur Edward Knoblock (1874–1945), an American by birth who lived in Worthing after 1918. Knoblock was one of the more notable furniture collectors of the age and the acknowledged pioneer of the Regency revival in England, owning important early nineteenth-century items from Thomas Hope's houses. He wrote enthusiastically and offered various items. He also wrote a little play for dolls for the Library, exclaiming, 'What a delicious house it will be when done.' He sent the committee a set of little prints and a 'tiny pack of playing cards I came across', adding nonchalantly, 'During my yachting trip I shall keep a look-out for any other suitable little articles.'

Lutyens continued to immerse himself in a great deal of detail. It was at his insistence that everything in the house was made to work, including the goods and passenger lifts, the electric lights and the major plumbing. He designed a sub-base on which the house could stand, containing drawers for dolls and overflow items, but also the electric generator and the water tank. The mechanical engineer was A.J. Thomas. Lutyens was also helped in providing working drawings by his draughtsman, F.B. Nightingale. George Muntzer, the head of a well-known West End firm of upholsterers and decorators, much used by Lutyens in his houses, was the honorary decorator.

Once the structure and architectural embellishments were complete, the Dolls' House was moved to Lutyens's own house in Mansfield Street, Marylebone, where it occupied the drawing room for two years

BELOW
The Dolls' House in
the drawing room in
Lutyens's own house in
Mansfield Street, London,
where the completed shell
stood for two years while
the furniture and contents
were assembled.

The house on display at the British Empire Exhibition at Wembley. It was there from April to November 1924. On the wall behind can be seen official souvenirs in the form of little china models by Cauldon Pottery. Here, the royal party, including Queen Mary and King George V, and the Duke and Duchess of York, are accompanied by Sir Edwin Lutyens (on the left).

while the furniture and other contents were assembled. Queen Mary took great personal interest, visiting frequently and once staying for over four hours, 'arranging and playing with everything'. The house was completed, with every item in place, 11 weeks before the opening of the British Empire Exhibition. It was unveiled to the press on 8 February 1924. The house left Mansfield Street in March, all the items being packed up in specially made wooden boxes, ready for the opening at Wembley in April, where it was put on display until November. During this period it was visited by no fewer than 1,617,556 people. The intention was then to exhibit the house permanently at Windsor Castle, in a former china store near the north entrance, adapted for the purpose.

At this stage, however, permission was requested to exhibit it at Olympia in 1925, for the *Daily Mail*-sponsored Ninth Ideal Home Exhibition. The *Daily Mail* commissioned a large Pilkington glass case in which to show the Dolls' House, and this second public exhibition gave Lutyens time to prepare the new space at Windsor for the house's ultimate reception.

All was ready by July 1925. The *Daily Mail* offered the new glass case from Olympia for the permanent display of the house, and it remains in the case today. It is of some historic interest in itself, as an example of Pilkington's 'flat' glass, a novel patent process that made possible the huge sheets of plate glass that were to become a feature of twentieth-century architecture, though not of Lutyens's architecture. The Dolls' House has remained at Windsor ever since, though the contents were taken to the Victoria and Albert Museum and the Science Museum for an overhaul in 1972. The room in which it is displayed has architectural features by Lutyens and murals painted by the fashionable decorative artist Philip Connard, who also worked on the *Queen Mary*. Due to the natural materials used in its construction, and its protection from daylight, the house is in an excellent state of preservation, both as a delightful period piece and as an increasingly interesting historical record – exactly as its promoters intended.

A detail of Lutyens's characteristic wall design in the Windsor exhibition room. The murals were painted by Philip Connard (1875–1958), well known at the time for his decoration of great ocean liners.

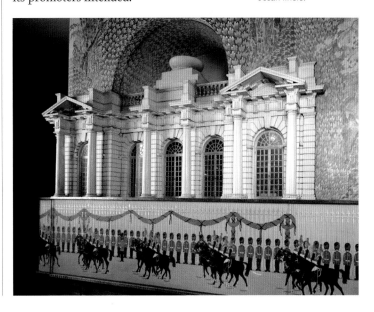

Tour of the Dolls' House

THE EXTERIOR

Queen Mary's Dolls' House stands on a black-painted sub-base, 0.61 metres high, designed by Lutyens, containing 104 cedar-wood drawers for storage, as well as the house's mechanical services. Above the base is a plinth that forms part of the house proper, containing in its basement the Wine Cellar. At either end are drawers containing the Garage and the Garden. The house has three main storeys. The exterior forms a detached case that can be raised up above the house by electrically powered machinery (hidden in the roof), revealing the interior.

Built to a consistent scale of 1:12, the principal elevations to north and south are 2.59 metres wide, and the side elevation is 1.49 metres wide. The house proper is 1.52 metres high to the top of the parapet. The plan of the house is an exercise in architectural symmetry and this is reflected in the exterior. It is a sign of Lutyens's intellectual rigour that there are only two blank windows on the outside and no unlit spaces within.

The north and south elevations pay distant tribute to Inigo Jones's Banqueting House in Whitehall and Wren's east and south fronts for Hampton Court Palace, key seventeenth-century English royal buildings, but they are not in any way direct copies. Lutyens had an incredible visual memory and his creative process was able to draw on features from any building he had ever seen, at an almost subconscious level.

There are two symmetrical chimney-stacks on the roof (not visible when the house is open), with flues to serve all the fireplaces in the house (all the main rooms have fires). The parapet is crowned with lead urns and statues. The four corner statues are the patron saints of the British Isles: St George and St Andrew (north), and St Patrick and St David (south). Over the centre of the north front is an angel bearing the Queen's crown. The other four figures are emblematic of Queen Mary's Christian names: Mary, Louise, Victoria and Augusta. They are all the work of the sculptor Sir George Frampton (1860–1928). The flagstaff flies Queen Mary's personal standard, with her arms, while the gilding of the glazing bars adds a final royal touch. All the sashes are double-hung and can open. Finally, the four sentry boxes have guards' instructions inside, copied from those at Buckingham Palace.

ABOVE
Though the façades are built of wood, painted to resemble Portland stone, the roof itself is made of real Welsh slates, cut to tiny proportions.

BELOW
Inigo Jones's Banqueting House of 1619 in Whitehall. This seventeenth-century royal building was one source of inspiration for Lutyens, with its alternating triangular and segmental pediments over the windows, and frieze of carved swags between the capitals of the columns.

ENTRANCE HALL

Having entered the ground floor through the main glazed door in the middle of the north front, the visitor is in the Entrance Hall, with Lutyens's staircase straight ahead. This is spatially the most impressive part of the house, rising through the three storeys, with arched lobbies to either side at ground and first-floor level. In plan, it is a perfect square of 50.8 centimetres. At ground-floor level the walls are lined with white and pinkish marble, while the stairs are pure white, and the floor is an ingenious pattern of alternating squares and diamonds of white marble and blue lapis lazuli. (The Indian government gave a batch of 20 different coloured marbles for use in the house.)

The staircase itself is a characteristic Lutyens design, whereby the bottom step is two-thirds the width of the room, and the lower flight then tapers to the narrower width of the upper flights. The silvered balustrade, inspired by Jean Tijou's (*fl. c.*1689–1712) ironwork at Hampton Court Palace, was made and given by the leading Arts and Crafts metalworker, J. Starkie Gardner (1844–1930), who also worked at the Palace of Holyroodhouse in Edinburgh. The underside of the landing was painted with the heavens and 12 signs of the zodiac, in

LEFT
Visitors' book, ink
stand and calendar
on the hall table.

blue, white and gold. The bronze statue of
Venus in the niche beneath the stairs is by
Francis Derwent Wood (1871–1926), who was
Professor of Sculpture at the Royal College
of Art from 1918 to 1923.

The furniture in the Entrance Hall
forms a good introduction to that found
throughout the house. The two lacquered
hall chairs (with the royal arms) and the
marble-topped side table were inspired by
the hall furniture at Blenheim Palace. The
longcase clock is a copy of a seventeenth-
century example by the famous clockmaker
Thomas Tompion (1639–1713). It is one of
seven clocks in the house made and
presented by Cartier, which are all capable
of keeping time. The two wrought-iron hall
lanterns with crowns were designed by
Lutyens. The suits of armour are among the
few objects in the house that seem slightly
out of scale. The painting of Windsor Castle
is by Sir David Young Cameron
(1865–1945), who became the King's

Painter and Limner in Scotland from
1933 to 1945.

Although the house has no guest rooms,
there is a visitors' book on the hall table,
with an ink stand, so that departing dolls
can sign their names. Glazed doors from
the lobbies to either side of the hall give
access to the secondary staircase to the left
(which serves all floors), and
to the passenger and service
lifts to the right. The
lobby leading to the
lifts has the hall
porter's chair, with
his copy of the
Daily Mail.

BELOW
The set of golf clubs laid
against a life-size ball.
The leather bag, which is
6.5 centimetres long, is
embossed in gold with
the royal cipher.

DINING ROOM

BELOW

The screen made by
Cartier out of Indian
playing cards.

The Dining Room, on the ground floor, overlooks the Garden. The walls were painted and gilded by George Muntzer's firm, which was responsible for all the house painting and upholstery. The overdoors are painted mainly in monotone grisaille, with vases and cherubs; and the ceiling panels, containing classical scenes of fauns, nymphs and satyrs, are by Professor Gerald Moira (1867–1959).

The oil paintings in the Dining Room include some of the finest in the house, especially the three on the fireplace wall, which are miniature copies of his own work by Sir Alfred Munnings (1878–1959), and depict the Prince of Wales (later King Edward VIII, r.January–December 1936) hunting, a prize Friesian bull and the King's charger, Delhi. The copy of Franz Xaver Winterhalter's (1805–73) *The Royal Family in 1846* is by Ambrose McEvoy (1878–1927), and the portraits of Edward III (r.1327–77) and James V of Scotland (1512–42) are by Sir William Llewellyn (1858–1941). The flower piece over the buffet is by W.B.E. Ranken (1881–1941). The smaller pictures in the lower tier include two views of King George V's coronation by Captain Pearse (a New Zealand artist) and two views of the state apartments at Windsor, also by W.B.E. Ranken. The long panel under the 'Winterhalter' is by the portrait painter Glyn Philpot (1884–1937).

The furniture is also distinguished, and reflects early eighteenth-century English styles. The set of 18 walnut chairs have carved eagle's heads terminating their arms, and salmon-coloured leather upholstery.

The dining table extends to 50.8 centimetres when fully open. The carved buffet was designed by Lutyens, as was the tall, red-lacquer Indian screen, made by Cartier of real eighteenth-century Indian *ganjifa* playing cards, given by Edward Knoblock. The carpet, an imitation Aubusson, was made and presented by Ernest Thesiger (1879–1962), an actor and colourful man-about-town, who had a keen interest in needlework.

LEFT
Detail of a table setting, with silver by Garrard.

The table in the Dining Room is set for dinner. The linen tablecloth, with the royal cipher, Garter Stars, shamrocks and thistles (representing British orders of chivalry), was woven in Belfast on the pattern of those at Buckingham Palace. The silver dinner service (for 18) was made by Garrard (the Crown Jeweller), while the glasses are Webb's crystal and were given by Thomas Goode & Co. Ltd. The four silver wall sconces are copied from examples at Windsor Castle. The show silver on the buffet includes a Monteith bowl (a bowl with a detachable scalloped rim for holding glasses) and 'Elizabethan' cups and covers and coconut cups, many of them presented by the craftsmen who made them. The Garrard service (including extra pieces stored in the Strong Room) cost £280 and was paid for in cash by Sir Herbert Morgan, chairman of the Dolls' House Committee.

The door to the left of the chimneypiece, partly concealed by the Indian screen, leads to the Servery, Butler's Pantry and Kitchen.

LEFT
McEvoy's miniature version of Winterhalter's painting of Queen Victoria and her family. The original is at Buckingham Palace.

SERVICE ROOMS

BELOW
The Kitchen has a
non-slip woodblock floor,
clock, table and dressers.

The Service Rooms in the Dolls' House are very similar to those in other Lutyens houses, with cupboards, shelves and other fittings designed by the architect himself. They are among the most intriguing and amusing of all the rooms in the house.

SERVERY

The Servery, where food was kept warm, has wooden tables, a hot-plate and other essential equipment, including, interestingly, a cocktail shaker, which would then have been a novel detail in an English house, as drinking cocktails had only been introduced to England as a fashion from America after the First World War. (Hot canapés at parties were another American innovation of the time.) The Servery links directly and conveniently to the Butler's Pantry and the Kitchen, on the ground floor.

BUTLER'S PANTRY

The Butler's Pantry occupies the north-east corner of the house, with the Strong Room for plate on the mezzanine floor above (reached via the back stairs).

The pantry contains two sinks, with wooden draining boards, for washing the silver, glass and china. The best china, made by Doulton and presented by Thomas Goode, is stored in the cupboards below the sinks and includes four dinner services, two breakfast services, a dessert service and a coffee service. There are separate drying cloths for china and glass, and a roller towel. Decanters, water jugs and entrée dishes stand ready for filling. There is even a Minimax fire extinguisher fixed to the wall, ready for an emergency.

ABOVE
The cupboards in the Butler's Pantry, designed by Lutyens, with Doulton china and miniature wine glasses.

STRONG ROOM

The Strong Room includes most of the silver dinner service, a tea service on a silver tray with an Abercorn-pattern tea kettle, as well as additional display pieces, such as a gold Monteith bowl. There are also miniature copies of the Crown Jewels with real diamonds – a little joke on the part of the committee.

KITCHEN

The Kitchen, on the ground floor, has several Lutyens features, including the woodblock floor and the furniture. The floor is made of 2,500 tiny wooden blocks in a parquet pattern. Lutyens preferred wood blocks to tiles for kitchen floors, as they are less slippery. As would have been normal in kitchens of this period, the walls are tiled to half height. The furniture comprises painted wooden dressers and a large oak kitchen table designed by Lutyens, identical to one he used to have in his own house. The clock hanging on the wall above the fireplace is also a typical Lutyens design. The polished steel stove, with two ovens and separate hotplate and pastry oven, is a coal-burning model known as an English Range.

The Kitchen contains its own Doulton china service, marked with a K, and a wide range of equipment, including a copper *batterie de cuisine* and a mincing machine, weighing scales and coffee grinder (made by the Twining Model Co.), wooden rolling pin, mops, brushes and carpet sweeper, all still recognisable, if now rather old-fashioned. The house also possesses what was then a very modern device, an electric Hoover vacuum cleaner. Note the cat and other details, such as a mousetrap, little (ivory) mice and the W.H. Smith calendar. Many of the provisions in the Service Rooms – such as Colman's mustard, Cooper's marmalade and Lifebuoy soap – are still household names; they were all chosen by Lady Jekyll.

ABOVE
Gold moulds, hand whisk and mixing bowl, rolling pin and marble slab for pastry on the kitchen table.

BELOW
The Dolls' House cat, with three mice (in a humane trap).

RIGHT
Two of the Dolls' House
Doulton plates, shown on
the rim of a modern,
full-scale royal plate.

SCULLERY

The Scullery beyond the Kitchen was for washing the kitchen pots and pans, as opposed to the dining-room china, which would have been washed in the Butler's Pantry. It is fitted with sinks, wooden draining boards, cupboards, plate racks, scrubbing brushes, soap and towels.

LEFT
Three copper kettles from
the complete *batterie de
cuisine*.

LIBRARY

Occupying the full width of the west side at ground-floor level, 1.14 metres long and 0.53 metres wide, the Library is one of the more impressive spaces in the house, by reason of both its architecture and its

contents. It is lined with Italian walnut, including the fitted bookcases and the screens of fluted Ionic columns at either end, which Lutyens introduced to give interest to the space. The chimneypiece is of white marble and lapis lazuli. This room is, to some extent, like a London club, and appears to be a masculine den, with pipes and cigars, fencing foils and a gun cupboard. The 10-centimetre Purdey guns (the smallest ever made) are laid out, at King George V's own suggestion, on one of the folio cabinets, where they can be seen more easily. They were modelled on the King's own guns and donated by Athol Purdey; they came complete with a leather gun case and cartridge bag. Every surface in the Library is cluttered with bric-a-brac: photographs, 12 royal dispatch boxes, bronzes and a model of George III's (r.1760–1820) yacht, the *Royal George*. The walnut desk has pens, ink and writing paper. There are also newspapers and magazines, including *The Times*, the *Daily Mail*, *Country Life* and the *Field*, as well as others now extinct, including the *Strand Magazine* and the *Morning Post*. The safe under the gun cabinet contains an insurance policy for the house – a characteristic humorous touch.

LEFT
One of the folio cabinets, with open drawer to show the collection of mounted drawings and watercolours. On the left can be seen Lutyens's own design of the north elevation of the Dolls' House.

The ceiling was painted by William Walcot (1874–1943). The portraits in the room refer to Tudor patrons of the literary Renaissance, including Elizabeth I (r.1558–1603) (over the chimneypiece), a painting based on the Armada portrait at Woburn, and full lengths (on the side walls), after Hans Holbein the Younger (1497/8–1543), of Henry VII (r.1485–1509) by Frank Reynolds (1923–1983), and Henry VIII (r.1509–47) by Sir Arthur Cope (1857–1940).

The Library furniture, like that in the Kitchen, was also mainly designed by Lutyens, including the desk and matching pair of folio cabinets, and the red leather

LEFT
Detail of the gold-tooled leather bookbindings and shelf edgings, with the GMR cipher and the royal crown.

upholstered sofa and armchairs. However, the three silver chandeliers were inspired by those at the great Kent country house of Knole. The pair of terrestrial and celestial globes show the British Empire coloured

country at the present moment' (as described in Lucas's *Book of the Queen's Dolls' House Library*), there are also a number of old miniature printed books, including three Bibles, a Koran, sets of Shakespeare, an English dictionary, English histories, works by the famous Scottish poet Robert Burns (1759–96) and by Charles Dickens (1812–70), early nineteenth-century English miniature almanacs, miniature children's books in French, and the smallest book ever printed from type, *The Mite* (1891), published and presented by E.A. Robinson (1869–1935). All the volumes contain a bookplate specially designed for the house by Ernest Shepard (1879–1976), the illustrator of *Winnie the Pooh*. There are also miniature reference books, produced by microphotography, such as *Bradshaw's Railway Timetable*, *Whitaker's Almanac* and *Who's Who*, together with 50 volumes of music and miscellanea, such as a Sandringham Stud Book and two miniature stamp albums. The folio cabinets were designed to house the collection of watercolours, etchings and drawings by contemporary artists.

pink, at its final and widest extent in 1922. There are three Persian rugs and a moleskin hearth rug. Concealed in one of the cupboards is a wireless, then a very modern invention – King George V's first radio broadcast was the opening speech at the Wembley Exhibition. (Television only became widespread in English homes after the Second World War.)

The books form a collection of 300 volumes, all specially bound by seven different firms, most notably Sangorski & Sutcliff. Apart from the unique autograph works by contemporary authors to represent 'all that is best in the literature of this

ABOVE
The Dolls' House bookplate, designed by the illustrator Ernest Shepard.

HOUSEMAID'S CLOSET

LOBBY

MAN'S ROOM

LOBBY

HALL AND STAIRCASE

UPPER HALL

This splendid space on the first floor is a perfect cube, with each of its sides measuring 0.51 metres. It is distinguished by murals by Sir William Nicholson on the walls and cove of the ceiling. They depict Adam and Eve being expelled from the Garden of Eden by a thunderbolt, mainly in grisaille, apart from the pink figures of Adam and Eve themselves. The animals, or 'their pets', as Nicholson described them, are particularly jolly, with pairs of giraffes, elephants, lions, tigers, hippopotami and the like. It took longer than expected to complete, and Lutyens had to chivvy Nicholson to finish on time. White marble-lined arches lead to lobbies, and over the arches are bronze busts in roundels of Earl Haig (1861–1928) and Earl Beatty (1871–1936), prominent land and sea commanders during the First World War. These are the work of C.S. Jagger (1885–1937), a leading sculptor who worked on many 1920s war memorials. His masterpiece is the Royal Artillery Memorial at Hyde Park Corner. The white marble busts on Siena marble plinths are by Sir William Goscombe John (1860–1952), and show King Edward VII (r.1901–10) and Queen Alexandra (1844–1925).

SALOON

The left lobby of the Upper Hall gives access to the Saloon, the principal reception room, which fills the whole of the east side of the house on the first floor and rises into a high coved ceiling. As in the Dining Room below, the architectural inspiration is derived from Inigo Jones. The ceiling panels and cove were painted by Charles Sims (1873–1928), Keeper of the Royal Academy Schools from 1920 to 1926, to represent 'The children of Rumour with her hundred

tongues'. The coving has a lattice pattern in *trompe-l'oeil* and rather twentieth-century-looking nymphs. The doorcases, dado and cornice are all of white marble, while the walls are hung with 'Pavia pattern' rose-coloured silk damask, woven to a minuscule scale by the Gainsborough Weaving Company of Sudbury in Suffolk. It has now faded to a golden tone.

The furnishing of the Saloon shows the 1920s approach to the arrangement of a

LEFT
This elaborate Chinese lacquer cabinet, on gilded legs, was commissioned and presented by the Marchioness of Londonderry (1878–1959) and was a particular favourite of Queen Mary's.

BELOW
The central table of the Saloon has a genuine eighteenth-century *pietra dura* (hardstone) top.

drawing room, with 'Georgian' sofas, chairs and tables grouped in the centre of the room, rather than ranged round the walls, as they would have been in the eighteenth century. The principal seat furniture comprises two gilt sofas and various armchairs with needlework covers, and is copied from the Chippendale furniture at Harewood House in Yorkshire. (King George V and Queen Mary's eldest daughter, the Princess Royal, married the 6th Earl of Harewood in 1922.) The grand piano, based on Lutyens's own design for a piano made for the Paris Exhibition in 1900, was made by Broadwood & Sons, and its case was painted by T.M. Rooke (1842–1942).

Flanking the fireplace is a pair of gilt console tables with elephant's tooth tops. Other furniture in the room includes a red and gold lacquer cabinet on a stand – a copy of one then at Londonderry House in Park Lane, commissioned and presented by the

Marchioness of Londonderry. The carpet is a copy of a sixteenth-century Indian 'garden pattern' rug.

The paintings in the Saloon complement its stately architecture. The overdoors show architectural capriccios of ruins, painted by Lady Patricia Ramsay (1886–1974), grand-daughter of Queen Victoria. The four small landscapes on either side of the fireplace are by Adrian Stokes (1902–72). The principal display is of six full-length state portraits, 25 centimetres high, in identical carved and gilt Lutyens-designed frames, made by Amédée Joubert & Sons and paid for by Mrs Marshall Field of Chicago. They are of King George V and Queen Mary by Sir William Orpen (1878–1931); King Edward VII and Queen Alexandra by Sir John Lavery (1856–1941); and George III and Queen Charlotte by Harrington Mann (1864–1937), after those by Reynolds at the Royal Academy.

QUEEN'S APARTMENT

The remainder of the first floor is given over to the King's and Queen's Apartments, each comprising three rooms: a wardrobe or dressing room, a bedroom and a private bathroom. Lavishly appointed down to the smallest details, and the epitome of 1920s luxury, these are among the most remarkable rooms in the house.

BELOW
The dressing table, with diamond-framed looking glass and turquoise enamel-backed brushes.

LEFT
The Queen's Wardrobe
has a vaulted ceiling with
little saucer domes,
inspired by the aisles of
Wren's St Paul's
Cathedral.

QUEEN'S WARDROBE

A door from the Saloon leads straight into the Queen's Wardrobe, which can also be reached from the secondary staircase. This small but monumental space forms a pendant to the bathroom on the other side of the Queen's Bedroom. The ceiling was painted by Professor R. Anning Bell (1863–1933), with the five senses, four winds and four seasons. Along the sides are fitted clothes cupboards. There is a Chubb safe for jewels, and a parasol of the type used by Queen Mary, made by Briggs.

Above, on the mezzanine, is the Luggage Room, where suitcases, hat boxes and travelling trunks are stored.

QUEEN'S BEDROOM

This room is similar architecturally to the Saloon, with a high coved ceiling and two-tier chimney-piece of Inigo Jones inspiration, here of white marble and green jade. The walls are hung with silk damask, which was originally blue, but has now faded to a silvery grey. The Queen's Bedroom is a delightful evocation of civilised twentieth-century luxury. The tall 'Queen Anne' four-poster bed, with shaped and domed canopy and plumes of ostrich feathers at the four corners, was designed by Lutyens and inspired by the state beds at Hampton Court. The ceiling cove was painted by Glyn Philpot, with a dramatic skyscape representing night and day, and its rectangular central panel is lined with cloudy looking glass.

The portrait framed into the chimneypiece of is the Duchess of Teck (1833–97), Queen Mary's mother, and was painted by Frank Salisbury (1874–1962). The other portrait in the room is of Mary, Queen of Scots (1542–87), by Gerald Kelly (1879–1972). The furniture, in homage to Queen Mary, is redolent of her personal taste for 'antiques'. The carpet, a copy of an Aubusson, is 35 by 42 centimetres, and was woven by the Stratford-on-Avon School of Weaving. The cream lacquer cabinet on a stand is derived from a rare James II original. The large amboyna-veneered cupboard was copied from an example in the Lever Collection, while the little walnut table at the foot of the bed is a copy of a late seventeenth-century example (a period then much admired) in the Devonshire Collection at Chatsworth. The gilt Garter Star-pattern clock and barometer over the doors are again original designs by Lutyens himself. Comfortable chairs, a daybed, a writing desk and a fully decked dressing table, with diamond-framed looking glass, complete the furnishings, while every surface is covered with small *objets d'art*: tiny carved hardstone animals, bonsai trees and a blue enamel Cartier clock. The silver wall sconces, like those in the dining room, are modelled on those at Windsor.

ABOVE
Blue enamel Cartier clock, designed by Lutyens in the Chinese style.

QUEEN'S BATHROOM

The Queen's Bathroom repeats the St Paul's Cathedral aisle format of the Wardrobe, with saucer domes and arches. The floor is of mother-of-pearl and the walls are lined with ivory and green shagreen, an exotic material favoured by the Georgians for small objects such as *etuis* and snuffboxes, of the type collected by Queen Mary. The bath and wash basin are of alabaster, with silver taps. The ceiling was painted by Maurice Greiffenhagen (1862–1931) of the Glasgow School of Art, with a seascape dotted with fish and mermaids. All is ready for use, with soft towels and a range of essences and soaps supplied by the firm of J. & E. Atkinson. Tiny drops of water come out of the taps, and Lutyens is known to have taken pleasure in explaining the plumbing to Queen Mary.

RIGHT
Doorway in the King's
Bedroom, with
swan-necked pediments,
leading through to the
King's Wardrobe.

KING'S APARTMENT

The King's Apartment, like the Queen's, comprises a wardrobe/dressing room, bedroom and bathroom, to the same architectural format, but with more sombre and masculine colouring and furnishing. The provision of separate bedrooms for husband and wife had been a feature of the planning of upper-class English houses since the eighteenth century, when it was first introduced as a French fashion. Lutyens usually adopted this arrangement in his house plans, for instance at the British Embassy in Washington, where it caused problems for the first residents, Lord Howard of Penrith and his wife, who found it inconvenient and uncosy.

KING'S WARDROBE

The King's Wardrobe is lined with panelled cupboards, all painted white. By contrast, the vaulted ceiling was brightly decorated by Wilfrid de Glehn (1870–1951). The light fitting, in mother-of-pearl and ivory, was designed by Lutyens and is a pair to that in the bathroom, while on the round table rests a little ceremonial Field Marshal's sword, made by Wilkinson.

KING'S BEDROOM

This room is particularly beautifully proportioned and visually satisfying, with its subdued decoration. The walls were painted by George Plank, to represent panels of Chinese wallpaper. Plank also painted the central rectangle of the ceiling with one of the best jokes in the house. It looks like a trellis pergola with flowers, but is in fact a musical stave, with the first bars

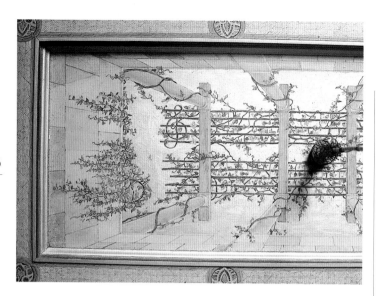

ABOVE
The ceiling of the King's Bedroom.

KING'S BATHROOM

The King's Bathroom has a vaulted ceiling, painted by Lawrence Irving (1897–1988) with satyrs and signs of the zodiac. On the walls are miniature *Punch* cartoons in red lacquer frames. The dado, bath and wash basin surrounds are all of green African verdite, while the floor is of white marble. The equipment includes tiny toothbrushes made by Addis, using the finest hairs available, from inside the ear of a goat, as well as bottles of manly hair-wash and rosewater.

of the National Anthem picked out on it in blooms.

The chimneypiece with Ionic columns is of black, white and Siena marble. Above it hangs a portrait of Princess Mary, The Princess Royal (1897–1965), by Ambrose McEvoy. The four-poster bed, designed by Lutyens, like that in the Queen's Bedroom, is also based on the Hampton Court state beds. It is hung with rose and gold silk damask, and its headboard, embroidered with the royal arms, is the work of the Royal School of Needlework. It was given by Princess Christian (1846–1923), Princess Marie Louise's mother, who was the founder of the school. The silver chandelier, copied from one at Knole, was made by Elkington & Co.

Other furniture in the room includes miniatures of late seventeenth- and eighteenth-century examples, mainly in walnut, including a pair of 'George I' chests of drawers and a pair of 'Chippendale' chairs, as well as comfortable armchairs and a sofa upholstered in rose and gold damask. The carpet was worked in petit point embroidery.

MEZZANINE AND TOP FLOOR

On the mezzanine levels in the corners of the house are six servants' rooms. These all have fireplaces and were comfortably furnished by Waring & Gillow. They are graded according to rank. The senior servants were provided with wooden beds with horsehair mattresses, while the juniors had iron beds with flock mattresses. All were provided with washstands, and the male servants have trouser-presses in their rooms.

The top floor of the house has two bathrooms and six principal rooms, some for servants and some for the family. The latter, reached by the passenger lift in the north-west corner, comprise the Princess Royal's Bedroom, the Queen's Sitting Room, the Night Nursery and the Day Nursery.

PRINCESS ROYAL'S BEDROOM

This is a simple, white-painted room, but is charmingly furnished with a chest of drawers, washstand and chairs decorated in late Georgian taste (illustrated above). A matching wardrobe stands in the lobby outside. The four-poster bed is 17.8 centimetres high and is a copy of the bed Lutyens designed for his own daughter (which, in turn, was inspired by that in Vittore Carpaccio's (c.1460–c.1525) painting *The Dream of St Ursula* of 1490–95). The set of 12 tiny framed prints showing 'The Cries of London' are antiques, presented to the house by Edward Knoblock. The pink Cauldon Pottery washstand set is similar to other sets in the servants' and children's rooms.

QUEEN'S SITTING ROOM

The Queen's Sitting Room, on the top floor of the Dolls' House, was intended to represent Queen Mary's personal tastes, including her enthusiasms for chinoiserie decoration, collecting small objects, such as oriental hardstone carvings, and needlework. The latter is indicated by an unfinished floral piece draped over the back of a chair.

The walls are hung with yellow silk, painted with water lilies by the famous illustrator Edmund Dulac (1882–1953).

The furniture is painted cream, lacquered in the Chinese taste, while the set of chairs simulates bamboo in the Georgian manner. The two glass display cabinets are scale models of Queen Mary's own at Buckingham Palace, and contain a collection of tiny jade and amber carvings of animals, including a water buffalo, a goat and a lion. There are also eight Egyptian amulets and a Siamese tobacco jar, while the rug is a copy of an eighteenth-century Chinese design.

RIGHT
The impressive cot for
the Prince of Wales in
the Night Nursery was
designed by Lutyens in an
impressively monumental
key, and was presented by
the banker, F.A. Koenig,
for whom the architect
was working at Tyringham
in Buckinghamshire.
It is made of ivory and
applewood, with a silver
trim. At the foot, an
obelisk supports a praying
angel, and at the head, an
octagonal canopy is
topped off with a coronet
and the Prince of Wales's
feathers.

NIGHT NURSERY

Next door to the Queen's Sitting Room, the Night Nursery contains a 'Chippendale' four-poster bed for Nanny and a cot for the Prince of Wales. The other furniture is no-nonsense, simple oak. Nanny's conservative tastes are hinted at by a portrait of Queen Victoria (by R.A. Pinks), a colourful flower piece (by F.M. Bennet, 1874–1952) over the fireplace, and *Bubbles* (after Sir John Everett Millais, 1829–96) by Alfred Hemming.

This room and its adjoining bathroom are equipped with a nostalgic array of baby products: Allenburys' rusks, chocolate, powdered milk and Vaseline, as well as a glass feeding bottle 2.54 centimetres long, baby soaps and a packet of Bromo lavatory paper.

ABOVE
The Nursery Bathroom is a much simpler
affair than the royal bathrooms downstairs.
The brightly painted scarlet chair is typical
of Lutyens's enthusiasm for strong colours.

DAY NURSERY

ABOVE
The Day Nursery has a wonderful array of children's toys, including a train set, model theatre and tiny car.

The Day Nursery, on the top floor, is a display piece of the classic age of English toys, with its train set, lead soldiers, model theatre (with a set for Peter Pan), hobby horse, dolls, Winsor & Newton paint box, chic wooden Pomona toys and an upright piano. The walls are colourfully decorated with scenes of nursery tales, again painted by Edmund Dulac. A modern feature of the time is the wind-up gramophone, with a set of 'His Master's Voice' records of the National Anthem, 'Rule Britannia' and 'Home Sweet Home'. In the lobby outside, glazed corner cupboards contain a nursery service by Wedgwood (marked with an N, to differentiate it from the kitchen set downstairs, marked K) and suitable provisions, such as cocoa, Huntley & Palmer biscuits, Nestlé's condensed milk and Tiptree jams.

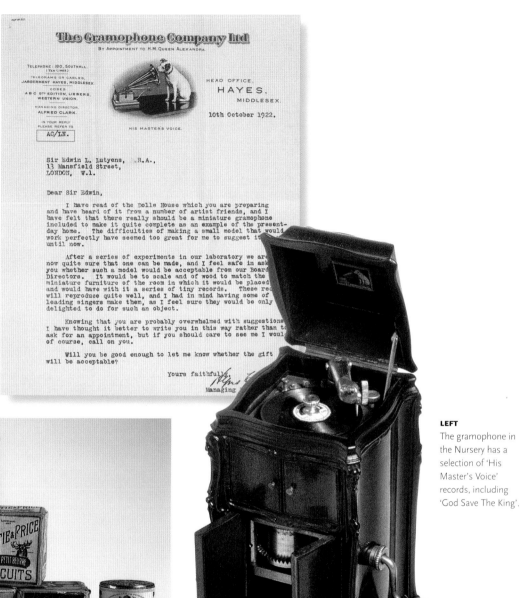

RIGHT
A letter from The
Gramophone Company
Ltd regarding the
miniature gramophone
for the Dolls' House.
Contributions like this one
were not requested, but
volunteered.

The Gramophone Company Ltd
BY APPOINTMENT TO H.M. QUEEN ALEXANDRA

TELEPHONE : 180. SOUTHALL.
(TEN LINES.)

TELEGRAMS OR CABLES.
JABBERMENT HAYES, MIDDLESEX.

CODES
A B C 5TH EDITION, LIEBERS.
WESTERN UNION.

MANAGING DIRECTOR.
ALFRED CLARK.

IN YOUR REPLY
PLEASE REFER TO
AC/LN.

HIS MASTER'S VOICE

HEAD OFFICE,
HAYES,
MIDDLESEX.

10th October 1922.

Sir Edwin L. Lutyens, R.A.,
13 Mansfield Street,
LONDON, W.1.

Dear Sir Edwin,

I have read of the Dolls House which you are preparing
and have heard of it from a number of artist friends, and I
have felt that there really should be a miniature gramophone
included to make it quite complete as an example of the present-
day home. The difficulties of making a small model that would
work perfectly have seemed too great for me to suggest it
until now.

After a series of experiments in our laboratory we are
now quite sure that one can be made, and I feel safe in asking
you whether such a model would be acceptable from our Board of
Directors. It would be to scale and of wood to match the
miniature furniture of the room in which it would be placed
and would have with it a series of tiny records. These records
will reproduce quite well, and I had in mind having some of our
leading singers make them, as I feel sure they would be only too
delighted to do for such an object.

Knowing that you are probably overwhelmed with suggestions
I have thought it better to write you in this way rather than to
ask for an appointment, but if you should care to see me I would,
of course, call on you.

Will you be good enough to let me know whether the gift
will be acceptable?

Yours faithfully,
Managing

LEFT
The gramophone in
the Nursery has a
selection of 'His
Master's Voice'
records, including
'God Save The King'.

ABOVE
Tins of Huntley & Palmer and McVitie &
Price biscuits, and Fry's cocoa were among
the provisions selected by Lady Jekyll.

SERVICE ROOMS

The east side of the top floor, served by the back stairs, contains the Housekeeper's Bedroom, the Linen Room and the Housemaids' Closet. (The men-servants' bathroom is on the mezzanine level, below.) These rooms are an accurate record of early twentieth-century domestic arrangements, now largely superseded by the labour-saving inventions of the past century.

The large, handsome Linen Room, with an early Georgian-style marble fireplace, has six large, panelled oak cupboards fitted round the walls. In the centre is a Lutyens table, similar to that in the Kitchen. A wicker laundry basket can be spied under the table, ready to take used items to a commercial laundry. 'Modern' inventions are present in the form of an early electric iron and a classic Singer treadle sewing machine. The cupboards contain a complete collection of household linen: tablecloths and napkins, towels and drying cloths, sheets and pillowcases.

These top-floor Service Rooms are completed by the Housemaids' Closet, which contains two sinks, copper hot-water cans and an array of cleaning materials, such as Lux soap and Vim, as well as mops and brushes. Another modern invention can be spotted, in the form of a classic Hoover vacuum cleaner. Even a utilitarian space like this was handsomely treated by Lutyens, and the splashback above the sinks is covered with miniature replicas of blue-and-white Dutch tiles, of which he was very fond and which he often used in his houses.

LEFT
The Housekeeper's Bedroom is typical of the rooms provided for the upper servants, with neat, modern furniture of unstained holly-wood from Waring & Gillow, and colourful washstand sets from the Cauldon Pottery.

BELOW LEFT
An American invention, the Singer sewing machine became a standard feature of many homes between the wars.

OPPOSITE
The linen in the Linen Room was all woven in Belfast and comprises complete sets of bed linen and table linen – painstakingly embroidered with the royal cipher *GRI*.

BELOW
The Housemaids' Closet.

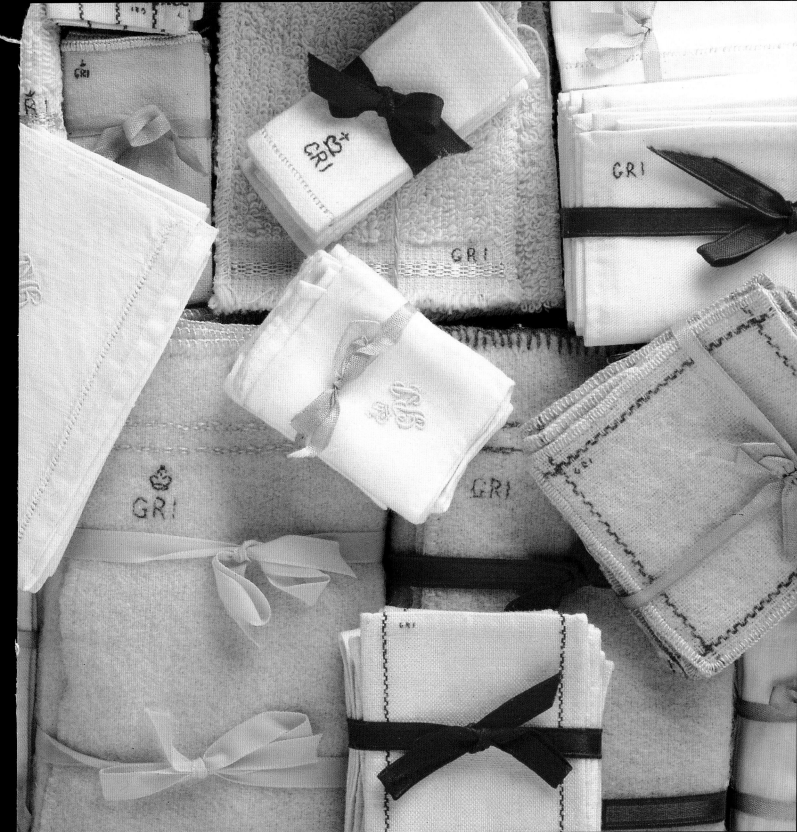

RIGHT
Cellar equipment for
decanting wine, including
a tiny corkscrew.

BELOW
As well as wine, the cellar
contains cases and casks
of Bass beer, including
Pale Ale and King's Ale.

54

BASEMENT

WINE CELLAR

The Wine Cellar is a large, groin-vaulted
space at basement level and was
stocked by Francis Berry of Berry Bros, the
St James's wine merchants (still happily
flourishing), with a splendid selection of
vintages. The tiny bottles were blown by the
Whitefriars Glass Co., and authentic labels
reproduced by microphotography. There is
also bottled and barrelled beer from Bass at
Burton upon Trent. The cellar is replete
with all the necessary equipment, including
corkscrew, funnel and a cellar book, which
lists the contents.

ABOVE
The Wine Cellar was
stocked by Berry Bros of
St James's Street.

GARAGE

The Garage, in its basement drawer, occupies the basement at the west end of the house. It contains six cars, all painted in the black and maroon royal livery. They represent the great British motor manufacturing companies of the 1920s: Daimler, Rolls-Royce, Sunbeam, Vauxhall and Lanchester. In addition, there is a Rudge motorcycle and a Rudge bicycle, a fire engine, and petrol pumps and cans.

BELOW
A Rudge motorcycle and sidecar parked by the petrol pump.

55

BASEMENT

RIGHT
Box-edged beds and
flower pots, brimming
with roses, irises and
lilies. The garden benches
designed by Lutyens are
still in production today.
The garden implements
include a little wheel-
barrow and a hosepipe
for watering the flowers.

BELOW
The garden roller, hoe
and rake, beside one of
Lutyens's classic garden
benches.

The Garden lies below the Dining Room and Saloon windows, and folds up ingeniously to fit into one of the basement drawers. It was designed by Gertrude Jekyll, doyenne of English gardeners. There are lawns (of green velvet), dwarf hedges of box (painted rubber) and flower beds filled with blue and purple irises, standard roses, lilies, carnations, sweet peas, poppies, marigolds, mallows and gentians, all modelled in painted metal by Miss Beatrice Hindley. There are also agapanthus in Italian terracotta pots, and hydrangeas and rhododendrons in wooden tubs. *Magnolia grandiflora* is trained against the side walls, and climbing roses range over the basement walls of the house. Six cypress trees (made out of real twigs from Dartmoor) stand sentinel along the front. Lutyens features

include miniatures of his classic garden bench and the wrought-iron entrance gates. A tiny bird's nest with eggs, a snail and even butterflies can be found amidst the planting – miniature and fitting grace notes to the meticulous detail and gentle humour found throughout the Dolls' House.

BELOW
The irises and roses were
painstakingly made in
painted metal by Miss
Beatrice Hindley, a friend
of Gertrude Jekyll's.